Tiered Activities
For Learning Centers

Differentiation in Math, Language Arts, Science & Social Studies

By

Dr. Karen Meador

©2005 Pieces of Learning
CLC0310
ISBN 1-931334-29-3
www.piecesoflearning.com
Illustrated by Greg Lawhun, Dodie Merritt
Printed in the U.S.A.

Table of Contents

Centers and Major Focus

Dedication

This book is dedicated to my adult children Kim Meador and Brad Meador who never complained about trying new exercises and activities I created. They both continue to demonstrate to me the grand capacity of the human creative spirit, and I delight in the unique ways they use their intellect and talent.

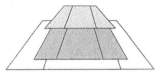

WHAT is This Book About?

This book is about learning centers and the learning opportunities they provide for students of varying ages and abilities. It provides information about the multiple types of centers and suggests the reasons for using centers. In addition, it makes a case for using tiered or differentiated centers in the classroom.

Tiered Activities for Learning Centers provides tiering suggestions for personalizing the centers for older or more able students and younger or less able students. The Tiering the Center section of each description allows teachers to use the centers at various grade levels even when the typical center is not appropriate for a particular age.

WHO is This Book For?

The centers in this book are appropriate for kindergarten through fifth grade students. Teachers of older students have also adapted many of the centers for use in middle school.

Educators in the following roles find these centers useful:

- Kindergarten and elementary classroom teachers
- Special education teachers
- Teachers of gifted students
- Resource teachers
- *Bilingual teachers
- Adults involved in home-schooling

*Bilingual teachers will appreciate several centers in which the activities' products are primarily oral.

HOW Can I Use this Book?

This book offers many choices for educators and multiple opportunities for students. Use the centers exactly as described or adapt them to include additional standards and objectives.

Think of Tiered Activities for Learning Centers as a centers' cookbook in which you may use the original recipes and then modify the ingredients based on individual taste.

The centers can be an integral part of instruction, a way to provide enrichment in the classroom, or a learning place where students go after completing or compacting out of their other work. Educators may use one tier of a center or use multiple tiers within the same classroom.

WHEN?

Many educators use centers on a regular basis every day. Others select one or two days a week to employ centers while a few simply use them occasionally. The objectives and the specific reasons an educator chooses to use this learning environment determine the frequency of the use of the centers. Reasons to Use a Center explains these reasons.

I hope MY teacher uses centers this year!

Common Myths about Learning Centers

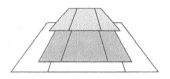

1. Students always make things in centers.

Fact: Students gather information, practice basic skills, plan, execute inquiries, and much more in centers. Students do not always produce a tangible product at a center.

Examples:
- Tape record student comments or a topical discussion between pairs or a small group of students.
- Set up a center where students can gather information or practice a skill needed for a class activity.

2. All centers are easy.

Fact: Centers need to be challenging enough to engage the thinking processes of children with various abilities.

Author's Note: Create centers with multiple levels or tiers in order to challenge varying abilities within the same class.

3. Centers should be used solely in the primary grades.

Fact: The use of centers is worthwhile in any grade and any subject. University graduate classes successfully use centers.

Author's Note: Some teachers of elementary students use the term station rather than center. Primary teachers could use stations to represent the centers with designated tasks and centers to represent those that are open-ended such as the housekeeping and blocks centers.

4. No teacher instruction takes place at a center.

Fact: Teachers instruct by continually asking questions while students are involved in work at centers. This helps to guide and frame learning. A teacher may also sit at an instructional center delivering a lesson as students rotate through the centers.

Author's Note: A straightforward example of a teacher-led center is located in the section titled <u>Large and Small Group Instruction</u> under the <u>Management Examples</u> in this book.

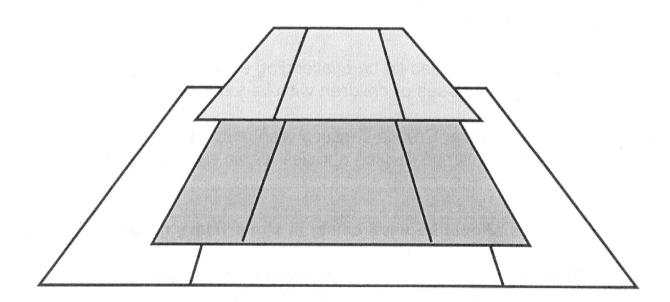

Reasons to Use a Center

1. To build student autonomy

2. To encourage pair or small group collaboration without the entire class being in groups at one time

3. When there is a shortage of materials or tools

4. When there is a need for continued use or exploration of specific materials/tools

5. When it is important to provide a learning experience in a different format

6. To facilitate the development of student interests

7. When there is a need for differentiation

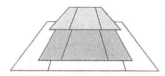
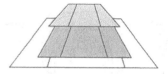

Planning Centers

Types of Center Activities

- lesson extensions
- skills practice
- preparation for upcoming theme or lesson
- resource/materials research
- interest explorations
- discovery/inquiry explorations
- work-in-progress

Ways to Arrange a Center

- **in specific corners or classroom sections**

   Shelves or partitions can separate small areas from the rest of the room. Students may spend a specified amount of time in the center or use it for "free choice."

- **on fold-up project boards**

   Project boards are available at most school and office supply stores. Since they are easily set up and then removed, project boards are advantageous when the room size is not appropriate for larger centers.

- **in a folder**

   All materials for the activity are contained in a folder that the student may work with at a desk, a table, or on the floor. Students usually complete the activities in one fairly short time period, and they often keep folders in boxes or plastic bags for easy retrieval.

- **in a plastic bag or paper sack**

   All materials for the activity are in a bag or sack for use anywhere in the room. Often, students complete the activities in a short period of time. You may store materials on skirt hangers and hang them on a peg-board or in a closet. (For examples see *It's in the Bag*, Meador, Pieces of Learning 1999.)

- **in a bucket, plastic tub, or shoebox**

These are easily stacked for storage and may be used anywhere in the room. A student may "check out" a box for two or three days and keep his/her center work in it.

- **as a wall display**

There is usually some sort of informative display at this center. It may include pocket charts with materials for students to gather and work on at their desks or serve as a resource where students get information for work in another part of the room.

- **inside a cabinet or drawer**

Adhere display information to the inside of cabinet doors and place a small box or basket of needed materials for the center inside the cabinet.

- **under a table or desk**

Put a poster display or other information on the underneath side of a tabletop. Place a pillow and flashlight under the table for student use. Students lie on their backs while investigating the information.

- **in a backpack**

Backpacks provide enough space to carry plenty of manipulatives or other objects and you may easily hang them for storage.

- **in a suitcase**

Suitcase centers allow students to work anywhere. Small groups of students might take them outdoors on an environmentally-friendly day.

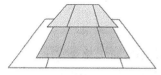

The Need for ►Tiered Centers

Do you ever dream in the summer before school starts that you will have a wonderful group of eager students the next year that will all be right on grade level? Alas, it is only a dream! In a heterogeneous group, some are not ready for grade level standards and objectives while others have knowledge and skills beyond those objectives. Unfortunately, since students vary in terms of learning needs, teachers must adapt to their diversity in skill level and learning styles in an effort to appropriately challenge each one.

The Vertical Classroom

Consider how your students might look if they were in a vertical classroom. In this classroom, the grade-level objectives/standards are at the midpoint of a vertical line from floor to ceiling as shown below.

The Vertical Classroom

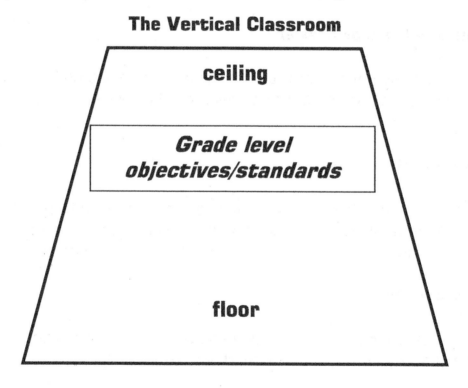

In the vertical classroom, students float up and down according to their ability to work on a particular educational objective/standard. Some students, those who are seated on the floor of this vertical classroom, are ill-prepared for the current learning objective.

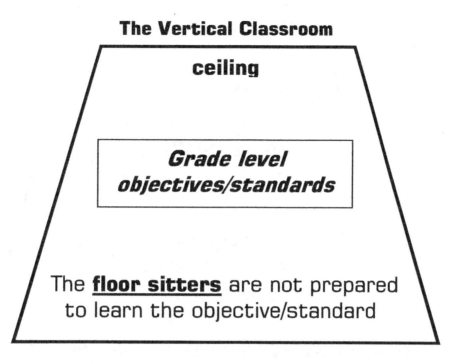

The Vertical Classroom

ceiling

Grade level objectives/standards

The **floor sitters** are not prepared to learn the objective/standard

Other students are ready for the objective/standard even though they have not yet accomplished it. These students float slightly below the middle in the vertical classroom.

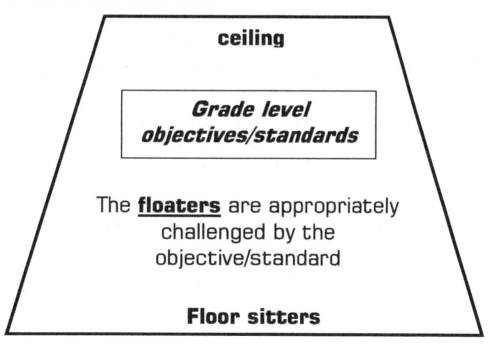

ceiling

Grade level objectives/standards

The **floaters** are appropriately challenged by the objective/standard

Floor sitters

Others may have some prior experience with the learning objective, but have not yet mastered it. They float just above the middle of the classroom, while a rare few of your students may have attached themselves to the ceiling because the learning objective is simply too easy for them.

The Vertical Classroom

The objective/standard
is too simple for the
Ceiling Huggers

The **High Floaters** have not yet
completely mastered the
objective/standard.

Grade level objectives/standards

Floaters

Floor sitters

Students do not always sit in the same position in the vertical classroom. For example, those who are Ceiling Huggers for one objective/standard may become the Floaters on another.

It is almost impossible to create a single-activity center that will appropriately challenge all of these students. While the floor sitters need simplification or scaffolding of the tasks related to the objective, the ceiling huggers need a much more complex task for mastery of the objective/standard.

One appropriate solution for this dilemma involves the development of multi-level tasks or **tiers** within a given center. These levels or **tiers** meet the needs of students from floor to ceiling.

Author's Definition: Tiered assignments are designed to facilitate learning for all students in a classroom regardless of experience, skill, or ability in the specific lesson content, process, and product. Tiered assignments are often based on a common objective but planned with specific students or groups of students in mind.

One objective and its concomitant learning activity may have multiple levels, or tiers, for student learning and involvement. Students work within the tier that best fits their needs. It is the teacher's challenge to provide all students with appropriate and interesting work in their tier.

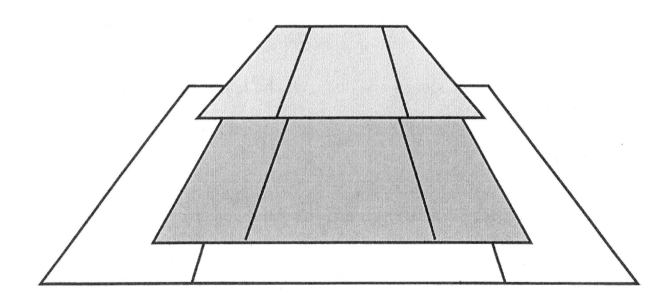

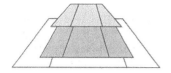 ▶ **Tiered Assignments**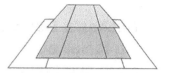

Ways to Differentiate

1. Change what the students **work with** (materials, tools, technology, etc.).

   Examples:

   - instead of reading from the textbook, able students read from a more sophisticated information source about the topic; while some students read and get information from a simple biography, others study a different, more challenging book about the same person

   - some students work with a pan balance to compare the weight of one object to another while others utilize weights to determine a more accurate measurement

2. Change what the students are doing or **the level** at which they are asked to think.

   Examples:

   - instead of analyzing the similarities and differences in the lives of George Washington and Abraham Lincoln, some students evaluate the relative importance of the actions of the two men

   - some students use number cubes to generate and then solve multiplication problems while a few employ the cubes to generate larger numbers for which they write numerous multiplication problems that yield the number as an answer

16

3. Change what students are **producing**.

Examples:

- some students create a class presentation about the scientist they studied, more able students gather appropriate reading for other students and then plan a Socratic questioning seminar on the topic

- most students complete a given logic problem while others write a "how to" that instructs others in the steps needed to solve the problem

4. Change the **objective.**

Examples:

- some students practice conversion of fractions to decimals as others explain the meaning of research data that is in decimal form

- although most students work on word processing skills at the computer, a few learn to use technology to draw graphs that represent data

**Look for the ▷ in the learning centers that follow.
It identifies tiered activities.**

Center Management

If the mere thought of having individuals or small groups of students engaging in a variety of different activities with different objectives at various locations throughout the classroom causes your head to spin, you may want to read this section several times.

Students do not come to the classroom knowing how to work in centers; they must be guided.

Do not assume students can do something you have not taught them!

Most groups of students need straightforward guidelines for traversing between centers and focusing within a center. Below are some suggestions for rules your students will need to practice. Different vocabulary would be required for younger students.

- Be considerate of others in your center and in the classroom.
- Focus on what you are supposed to do in the center.
- If you finish a center ahead of time check to be sure you did quality thinking and work. Then continue to explore the materials and opportunities in the center.
- If you have a question while working in a center, raise your hand until the teacher sees you. Then continue working on your own until help arrives. Do not leave the center or interrupt the teacher.
- Listen for directions about when and where to move when changing centers.
- Leave the center exactly the way the teacher set it up.

Educators may initially use centers that require a minimum of time for task completion in order to help students focus on appropriate center actions. Five to 10 minutes works well, depending upon the age of the students. Once they understand how to function in centers, gradually increase the time.

When difficulties arise, review center actions, and let students practice these through simulation. Students who cannot handle themselves in this format may work at a desk while observing the appropriate actions of others involved in centers. It may be helpful to use a tape recorder to capture student conversations at some centers. Students start the blank tape when they enter the center. They say their names and then simply leave the recorder running as they work at the center. The teacher can review the tape and share segments, if needed, with students who are wasting time while off task.

The grouping of students for center rotations depends on the educator's objectives. It is advantageous to group students homogeneously according to need. For example, if the teacher suspects two or three students need extra direction at a center, these students should move through the centers together. When they arrive at the center where they need assistance, the teacher can work with all of them together rather than watching for each individual student's group to arrive at that center.

The opposite also applies since it is helpful to group students with advanced knowledge or expertise for a center. The teacher can provide more advanced information or instruction when those students arrive at the center together.

Author's Note: The practice of grouping students heterogeneously for center rotations is inappropriate for advanced students who may find they are guiding other children rather than encountering their own challenging learning opportunity. Every child should have an opportunity for new learning at a center. Heterogeneous grouping may also adversely affect less able students who do not get an opportunity to think for themselves when others dominate the center.

Management Examples

Large and Small Group Instruction

Consider combining direct large and small group instruction with centers. Deliver large group instruction to the entire class followed by a specific assignment. Then divide the class into three groups. One group of students remains at desks or tables to work on the assignment that followed the large group instruction. Another group works in a specified center while the third group meets with the teacher who delivers small group instruction based upon student needs. The groups rotate until all have had an opportunity to be engaged in the three activities. Time spent

in each activity varies by grade level. As an example, first grade students function well when each activity takes about 15-20 minutes or less. Students rotate through all three planned learning opportunities in about an hour. For this type format, group students according to their needs relating to the objective for the teacher's small group instruction. A specific First Grade example follows on page 21.

A. Large Group Instruction Objective:

The student will demonstrate understanding of single digit subtraction.

Description: Following teacher instruction to the large group involving working with manipulatives to engage in subtraction and practice writing and answering subtraction problems, students receive a set of practice problems to work independently.

B. Small Group Instruction Objective:

The student will recognize and write vowel blends.

Description: The teacher works on vowel blends with a small group of students. The instruction and guided practice varies based upon the facility of the students with the objective and students with similar needs relating to this objective are grouped together. For example, students who are challenged with the oral sound of vowel blends work together with the instructor as they practice enunciating and writing selected blends. Later, when students who have a clear understanding and good articulation of vowel blends work with the teacher, they practice using the blends in words.

C. Center Objective:

The student will investigate patterns in nature.

Description: In this center students categorize multiple things collected from nature into groups based on specific patterns such as branching. They practice using magnifying glasses and/or microscopes.

Individualized Reading and Centers

Involve students in meaningful centers while arranging time to listen to individuals or pairs of readers. Set up four or five centers that will last for several days. Ask students to do quality work in as many centers as time permits. While some may complete all the centers, others may only do three or four. Centers can provide practice or extension of a previously learned objective or prepare students for an upcoming objective.

This makes it less critical for students to complete every center since the objective has or will be covered in another format.

Designate a set amount of time to devote to centers each day. While most students attend to these centers, ask individuals or pairs to read aloud for a short period of time. You can reach many students during this time by using the "readers in waiting" technique. Call three or four readers at a time. As one student or a pair read aloud, the waiters sit behind them until it is their turn. When waiters move into the readers' positions, the teacher calls other students from the centers to fill the waiters' positions. In this manner, little or no time is wasted between readers. Students move from the readers' positions back into the centers they left. Although it is usually impossible to hear all students in the class read on one day, it is relatively easy to hear them during a two-day centers' episode.

Centers for Differentiation

Arrange one or more centers for specified students. When the large group instruction is not appropriate for a few children, send them to a center based on their needs while the other students receive instruction. Other students may choose to go to this open center if and when they complete their work early, but the center is not assigned to them.

For example, the teacher covers the concept of addition of fractions during large group instruction. Through observation or pretesting, the teacher knows that one or two of the students already has good facility with this process and do not need the instruction or basic practice. While the large group instruction takes place, the knowledgeable student(s) works in a center that requires more sophisticated use of fractions. For example, the student might write an explanation of the process of adding fractions and then suggest how to use a similar process to subtract fractions. There would be an opportunity for completing word problems involving both addition and subtraction of fractions. Before the student begins the word problems, the teacher should check for understanding and provide instruction if needed.

Author's Note: Baggie centers are very useful for this more individualized purpose. (See *It's in the Bag*, Meador, Pieces of Learning. 1999.)

Learning Centers

**Differentiation in Math, Language Arts,
Science & Social Studies**

**Opposites
Attribute Socks
Morphing Around
Balancing Act
Double-Dipping
Ways to Measure
Research in a Bag
Background Music
Characterology
It's Inclined
Advertising Police
Elaboration**

Opposites

Standard Addressed
Language Arts: The student develops vocabulary to express ideas clearly.

Objectives
1. The student will develop an understanding of the concept of opposites.

2. The student will determine characteristics of objects.

3. The student will use flexible thinking in order to determine how one object can represent several terms.

Materials
Collection of objects
Opposites Mat

Student Directions
1. Place objects representing the words given on each section of the opposites mat. Be prepared to explain your choices.
2. Ask your teacher to check your work.
3. Remove the objects from the mat to get it ready for the next person.

➢ **Tiering the Center**

➢ **Older or More Able Students**

Select more advanced vocabulary for the opposites on the mat. For example, use the term *malleable* rather than *soft*. Provide a dictionary for student use at the center. Use fewer cells since the students will spend some time determining the meanings of the words. Since it may be difficult to find objects that fit all the words on the advanced mats, number the cells on the mat to make it more interesting. Once students have completed individual work and determined the meaning of the words in the cells, they can work with a partner taking turns rolling a number cube (die) to determine which cell will be explained to the partner. The partner can check the definitions and use of the words in sentences.

➤ Option 1

Use one simple and one advanced term in each cell. A student hypothesizes the meaning of the advanced term based on the meaning of the simple term. Dictionary use follows to determine accuracy of the hypothesis. The student makes an individual list of the advanced terms for the opposites. See the example on page 27.

➤ Option 2

Both the terms in each cell are advanced. (See example p.27).

➤ <u>Younger or Less Able Students</u>

Use fewer cells on the mat and simpler vocabulary (page 27) that you have discussed in class. Use the mat during large group practice before students attempt it independently. Provide objects for which the characteristics are very obvious.

Preparation of the Opposites Mat

There are several ways to prepare the mat.

(1) The quickest and easiest way is to write words that are opposites on each of several pieces of 8 ½ x 11 inch paper. Place them on a table or floor in a rectangular pattern. This method allows teachers to exchange the sets of words easily or differentiate the center based on the sets of words provided.

(2) A more durable mat can be prepared by drawing the rectangles with permanent marker on a plastic tablecloth or shower curtain.

Opposites Mat

long	soft	straight
short	hard	curvy
rough	small	light
smooth	large	heavy
tall	bright	noisy
short	dull	quiet

➤ Examples of Opposites Mats for Older or More Advanced Learners

➤Option 1

1 <u>petite</u> large	2 <u>noisy</u> muted	3 <u>wispy</u> huge
4 <u>lackluster</u> bright	5 <u>droll</u> fun	6 <u>competent</u> level

➤Option 2

1 diminutive substantial	2 deafening muted	3 wispy weighty
4 brilliant lackluster	5 marvelous abysmal	6 coarse level

➤ Example for Younger or Less Able Learners

1 straight curved	2 long short
3 smooth rough	4 hard soft

Attribute Socks

Standards Addressed
Science: The student develops an understanding of the properties of objects and materials.
Language Arts: The student develops vocabulary to express ideas clearly.

Objectives
1. The student will demonstrate the ability to determine the characteristics (attributes) of objects.
2. The student will practice resistance to closure by determining attributes rather than guessing the names of the objects.

Materials
1. dark colored socks
2. small objects than can fit in the socks (examples: empty contact lens container, soft ball, emery board, bell, a sealed box of paper clips, etc.)
3. tape recorder if needed

Prepare the attribute socks by placing one object in each sock and tying the top of the sock. The number of socks needed is based on the age of the students.

Student Directions
1. Practice your skills of observation using touch, smell, and sound.
2. Name the attributes of the object in each sock. Write these or tape record your list.
3. DO NOT try to guess the name of the object in the sock.
4. Compare your observations with another student.

➤ Tiering the Center

➤ Older or More Able Students
After students feel the socks, they categorize them into two or more groups based on attributes.

➤ Younger or Less Able Students
Place objects into the socks that have very distinct characteristics. For example, use a ball rather than a contact lens container.

Morphing Around

Standards Addressed
Math: The student computes fluently.
Language Arts: The student uses grammatical and mechanical conventions correctly.

Objective
The objective varies according to the type of morphological matrix that is used in the center.

Materials

1. Writing materials
2. Drawing materials (for some matrices)
3. Random number generator (die)
4. *Morphological Matrix

Student Directions
Directions vary according to the type of matrix used in the center and will be given separately for each matrix that appears in this book.

Author's Definition of a Morphological Matrix: A morphological matrix is composed of cells that may be combined in random order to create an interesting blend of elements. The rows of the matrix are numbered and a random number generator is used to select one element from each of the columns.

Example: **Story-Telling Morphological Matrix**

Student Directions Use the items in the cells rolled as components in your creative story. Your oral story should be more than three sentences. You can use the components in any order and add other things to the story. Tell the story to your partner or tape record it. As an example, if you rolled 3, 2, 5, and 1, the story would have the following components: a child crying loudly, at the park downtown, during the coldest night of the year, with a clown carrying an umbrella.

	Who	**Where**	**When**	**With**
1	a man with a cane	in the middle of a field of corn	after the sun went down	a clown carrying an umbrella
2	a teacher carrying a baby	at the park downtown	in the middle of a tornado	the woman in the long black dress
3	a child crying loudly	near the elephant cage at the zoo	before school started in the morning	a little girl named Susan who was mad at her brother
4	a cow chasing a rancher	on a busy highway	during a family reunion	the President of the United States
5	a person on roller skates	in the hall at our school	during the coldest night of the year	Shirley, a yellow dog with bows in its hair
6	a student with a heavy backpack	in the food court at the mall	during cartoons on Saturday	a friend with a broken leg

Language Arts   Morphological Matrix

Objective

The student will practice creating specified types of sentences.

Student Directions

1. Roll the random number generator (die) to select an element in each column.
2. Use the elements rolled in the first two columns to write the type of sentence you rolled in the last column. You may change the form of the verb to write your sentence correctly.
3. Repeat these steps until you have written at least three sentences.

	Noun	Verb	Type of Sentence
1	a horse	ran	question
2	Mr. Jones	moved	statement
3	the teacher	sat	exclamation
4	Jan	closed	question
5	my dog	fell	statement
6	a caterpillar	ate	exclamation

Language Arts   Morphological Matrix

Objectives

1. The student will demonstrate knowledge of a character from a book.
2. The student will practice using correct grammar and punctuation.

Student Directions

1. Roll the random number generator (die) to select an element in each column.
2. Read or listen to a tape recording of the book for the character you rolled.
3. Write a short creative story using the elements you rolled. Think about the characteristics and actions of the character in the book you read or heard and use these in your story.

	Character	Happening	Another Character
1	Max from Where the Wild Things Are	fell out of a tree	a friend
2	Eggbert, the Slightly Cracked Egg	was chased by a dog	parents
3	George from Curious George	was arrested	a baseball player
4	Harry from Harry the Dirty Dog	went for a ride on a train	the zoo keeper
5	Lottie from Lottie's New Beach Towel	went to school	a frog named Freddie

➤ **Tiering the Center   Morphological Matrix**

➤ **Older or More Able Students**

Alter the matrix on page 32 by selecting characters from more complex pieces of literature. For example:

	Character	Happening	Another Character
1	Reginald from The Bat Boy & His Violin	fell out of a tree	a famous football player who had broken his leg
2	Aunt Chip from The Great Triple Creek Dam Affair	was chased by a dog	a bus driver whose bus had a flat tire
3	Blue from Peach and Blue	was arrested	a singer who was afraid to perform
4	Luz from The Faralitos of Christmas	went for a ride on a train	a policeman helping someone who was lost

➤ **Younger or Less Able Students**

Use a picture matrix like the one on page 34 for story telling. Students may tell their story into a tape recorder or create a rebus story.

Bilingual Note: This method is also effective for students who are just learning to speak English.

Author's Note: Teachers can create a hands-on matrix by enlarging the cells and making each on a separate laminated piece of poster board. Use Velcro® to attach these to cells drawn on a large piece of poster board. Students may then remove the cards for the cells that they rolled with the random number generator (die). As students tell their story, they can arrange the cards in the proper order to practice story sequencing.

Picture Matrix

	WHO	WHERE	WHEN	ACTION	WITH
1	DOCTOR	AT THE BEACH	IT WAS RAINING	RUNNING	DOG
2	GOLPHER	IN THE MOUN-TAINS	IT WAS HOT	SWIMMING	PRESIDENT
3	BRIDE	AT THE GROCERY STORE	AT NIGHT	LAUGHING	TEACHER
4	RABBIT	AT HOME	WHILE SLEEPING	CRYING	FIREMAN
5	GORILLA	AT THE CIR-CUS	ON THE 4TH OF JULY	GETTING MAD	TRUCK DRIVER

Mathematics   Morphological Matrix

Objectives

1. The student will practice computation skills.
2. The student will practice using a variety of ways to solve problems.

Student Directions

1. Use the random number generator (die) to select a cell from each column.
2. Work the problem you rolled and show your answer using the method rolled in the last column.
3. Create and answer at least 3 problems.

	numeral	computation	numeral	way to show answer
1	12	+	5	as a picture
2	8	-	7	with manipulatives
3	10	X	4	equation
4	7	+	6	in words

➤ **Tiering the Center**

➤ <u>**Older or More Able Students**</u>

Use the matrix to generate your own two-step mathematical problems.
Write and solve the equation. Complete at least 5 different equations.

	Numeral	Computation	Computation	Computation	Numeral
1	6	+	3	-	6
2	7	-	4	X	5
3	5	+	1	+	3
4	8	+	2	X	4
5	9	-	5	+	7

➤ <u>**Younger or Less Able Students**</u>

Use the matrix to create your own mathematical problems. Write the
problem and find the answer. Complete 5 different problems.

	Numeral	Computation	Computation
1	5	+	4
2	8	-	3
3	6	+	5
4	9	-	2

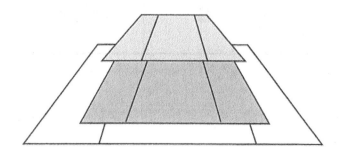

Mathematics   Morphological Matrix

Objective
The student will practice numeral, color, and shape recognition.

Student Directions
1. Roll the random number generator (die) to select a cell from each column.
2. Draw what you rolled. For example, you might draw 4 blue triangles.
3. Do #1 and #2 several times.

	Number	**Color**	**Shape**
1	6	blue	△
2	4	red	◯
3	5	green	☐
4	2	orange	▯
5	3	yellow	☆
6	7	purple	▱

Science   Morphological Matrix   Create an Animal

Objectives
1. The student will consider how specific physical attributes affect an animal.
2. The student will practice thinking creatively.

Student Directions
1. Create a new animal using the cells you roll with the random number generator (die).
2. Draw the animal and give it a name.
3. What does it eat? Where does it live? How did it get these strange features? (Be prepared to explain your answers.)

	Head	Body	Tail	Legs
1	pig	whale	cow	turtle
2	alligator	donkey	pig	crane
3	bear	cow	monkey	tiger

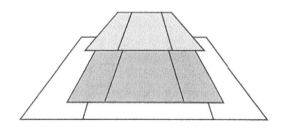

➤ **Tiering the Center**

➤ **Older or More Able Students**

	Head	Body	Tail	Legs	Other
1	pig	whale	cow	turtle	turtle shell
2	car	donkey	deer	crane	eagle wings
3	bear	cow	monkey	rhinoceros	porcupine spikes

➤ **Younger or Less Able Students**

Provide pictures of these animals.

	Head	Body	Tail
1	**cat**	**rabbit**	**dog**
2	**dog**	**cat**	**rabbit**
3	**pig**	**dog**	**pig**
4	**rabbit**	**pig**	**cat**

> **Advanced   Morphological Matrix   Create an Animal**

Student Directions

1. Create your own creature by rolling the random number generator (die) for a component in each of the columns. Use the information in the cells you rolled to create the creature.
2. Draw your creature.
3. Give the creature a name.
4. Explain where the creature would live in terms of climate and location based upon its attributes. Be sure to justify your answer based upon what you have learned in class.
5. Discuss how it uses its defense mechanism to avoid predators.
6. Based upon the creature's size, what do you anticipate will be its predators? Justify your answers based on knowledge of the types of living things that are in the habitat in which your creature lives.
7. Provide any other important information about your creature.

	Color	Shape	Body Length	Type of Feet	Reproductive System	Defense Mechanism
1	brown	oblong	2 feet	hooves	soft eggs	venom
2	free choice	cubic	6 feet	webbed	hard eggs	spines
3	green	oblong	8 inches	crow	live birth	claws
4	yellow	cylindrical	2 inches	none	free choice	camouflage

Balancing Act

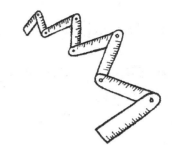

Standard Addressed

Science: The student uses scientific inquiry to gather information.

Objectives

1. The student will develop an understanding of the concept of balance.
2. The student will determine how weight affects balance.

Materials

1. Empty 1-pound coffee can
2. Yardstick
3. Various sizes of bulldog paper clips
4. Drawing/writing materials

Center Preparation

Turn the coffee can on its side and use masking tape to secure it to a table or desk so that it will not roll.

Student Directions

1. Balance the yardstick on the coffee can as if it were a seesaw. Draw a picture showing the location of the coffee can with the yardstick. Write the number on the yardstick that tells where the coffee can is located. For example, is the coffee can right below the number 15 on the yardstick?
2. Attach one of the paper clips to one end of the yardstick, and then balance it on the coffee can. Now what number is the coffee can below on the yardstick? Draw a second picture including the number where the coffee can is located.
3. Add another paper clip to the same end of the yardstick and find out how this extra weight affects balance. Draw a third picture.
4. Write a brief explanation of your findings.

➤ **Tiering the Center**

➤ <u>**Older or More Able Students**</u>
Objectives
1. The student will develop an understanding of the concept of balance.
2. The student will consider multiple variables in an experiment.

Materials
1. Empty 1-pound coffee can
2. Cans with Various Circumferences (vegetable can, larger coffee can, etc.)
3. Wooden Ruler
4. Thin, flexible ruler or other straight edge

Student Directions
1. Create your own experiment to find out how weight affects balance using the materials provided in this center. Is it possible to balance the yardstick with varying weights on both ends?
2. Report your findings in writing.
3. What other variables besides weight could you consider in this experiment? Try at least one additional variable and report your findings.
4. Do any of these variables make a difference?

➤ <u>**Younger or Less Able Students**</u>

Materials
1. Same as original center (1-4 page 41)
2. Tape recorder

Student Directions
1. Balance the yardstick on the coffee can as if it were a seesaw. Draw a picture showing the location of the coffee can with the yardstick.
2. Put one of the paper clips on one end of the yardstick and then balance it on the coffee can. Draw a picture showing what happened.
3. Add another paper clip to the same end of the yardstick. Draw a third picture.
4. Tape record your description of what you did in this center and what happened.

Double-Dipping

Language Arts: The student uses reading skills and strategies to interpret texts.

The Double-Dipping idea does not necessarily have to be used in a center. However, it is advantageous in this format when students need to share books and other materials.

Double-Dipping works as a menu through which students make choices about the manner in which they will respond to text. Students build their own double-dip ice cream cone by selecting one paper cone that has the name of a book on it and two paper scoops of ice cream. Each scoop of ice cream asks students to respond in a unique way to the text. Different flavors (colors) of ice cream designate different types of questions or responses. For example, questions or activities about characters such as "describe the main character" and "tell how you are like the main character" should be written on the same flavor (color) ice cream. Questions or activities pertaining to the plot or main idea would be written on another ice cream flavor. Then, as students select one scoop of each flavor, the activities will vary.

Objectives

The objectives for this center vary according to the particular book selections placed in the center. For example, a collection of nonfiction books about sports figures might lead students toward an understanding of the need for cooperation and teamwork. You might use a set of fictional picture books so that students could practice literature skills such as character analysis and main idea.

Materials

Books   Ice cream cone cutouts or patterns
Paper bowls   Small basket
Scissors   Glue
Paper
Printed scoops of ice cream on various colors of paper

Center Preparation

1. **Select an** appropriate number of books for the center based upon your objective. It is advantageous to provide one or two books more than the number of students working at the center at one time in order that everyone has a choice. If there are too many choices, students spend their time deciding what to read rather than completing the center tasks.
2. Print the questions on colored paper scoops, cut them apart, and place them in bowls according to color. Print several copies of each set. Sample scoops are provided on pages 47-50.
3. Prepare the cones in the same manner, and place them in a small basket or box (you may print the name of a book on each cone or ask students to write these after making a selection). A pattern for the cones is provided on page 46.
4. Optional: It may be advantageous to prepare a poster for the center displaying the choices of questions/activities for each ice cream flavor. This will alleviate the need for students to dig through all the scoops in the bowls as they decide what they want to do.

Student Directions

1. Briefly look at the books provided in the center. Then select one that you will read and work with.
2. Write the name of this book on one of the ice cream cones provided.
3. Read the book.
4. Select one paper scoop of ice cream from each of two flavors (colors), and glue these on paper to make your double-dip treat. Be sure to put your name on the paper.
5. Answer the questions or complete the activities on the scoops and attach these to your ice cream cone.

➤ Tiering the Center

The tiering of this center is an example of the differentiation method of changing the materials with which the students work. Tier this center by selecting books for students based upon individual abilities. Less able or younger students work with books slightly below their reading level while more able or older students work with books that are somewhat challenging. This method allows all students to think at a high level of Bloom's Taxonomy as opposed to asking some to respond to a low level question. When less able or younger students work with texts slightly below their comfortable reading level, they can utilize their energies on question response rather than struggling with the reading. It is vital that all students have ample practice using higher order thinking skills rather than simply recalling facts from texts.

➤ <u>Older or More Advanced Learners</u>

Select texts with rich plot, complex character interaction, or advanced vocabulary.

➤ <u>Younger or Less Able Students</u>

Select texts that are slightly below the student's reading level in order that the student can focus on the literary skills required for question response.

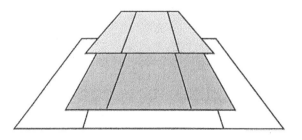

"Scoop" Questions for Fiction Books

Patterns for "Scoop" Questions

Print on strawberry (pink) paper

Write three to five sentences that tell the most important part of the story.

Write three to five sentences that explain one of the problems in the book.

Write what you would tell a friend who asked you how this book was different from other stories.

Write three to five sentences that explain the theme of the story.

Print on chocolate (light brown) paper

List five to eight words that the author used to describe one of the characters.

Write two or three sentences that describe something the main character <u>did</u> in the story.

Who was the main character in this book? Write one or two sentences that describe that character.

Describe ways in which you are both like and unlike the main character.

Print on vanilla (white) paper

Make a list of three or four action words (verbs) in the book. Explain which of these words told about the most interesting action in the story.

Find and write at least five words that the author uses to describe something in the book. Use one of them to describe something you own.

Make a list of at least five words from the book that you want to use in your own writing. Use at least one of these in your own new sentence.

Find and copy one entire sentence that the author uses to describe something in the story. Use part of this sentence to describe something else.

Explain what you would have done if you had been added as a character in this story.

Describe something that you believe happened to one of the characters after the story ended.

Tell how the story might have been different if it had taken place in your town.

Describe something that could have happened to one of the characters before this story began.

Ways to Measure

Standards Addressed

Math: The student applies appropriate techniques, tools, and formulas to determine measurements.

Math: The student uses the language of mathematics to express mathematical ideas precisely.

Objectives

1. The student will develop concepts of measurement including weight, height, length, and width.
2. The student will understand how to use various measurement tools including a ruler, yardstick, bathroom scales, and balance.
3. The student will practice using the language of mathematics.

Materials

1. Card Set 1 - Create on blue card stock and cut out
2. Rebus Guide – Create one on white paper for each student
3. Picture Set for Rebus Work – Create one on white paper for each student
4. Measurement tools:
   - ruler
   - yardstick
   - bathroom scales
   - pan balance and weights
   - string
   - other tools as needed
5. Objects to measure (these will vary according to the child's age/ability)
6. pencil
7. medium-sized wooden building block
8. marble
9. paper sack

Student Directions

How do you know what tool to use to measure something? For example, what should you use to measure weight? With the help of the objects and tools in this center, you can figure it out.

1. Match the colored cards in this center with the measurement objects provided. These include the ruler, yardstick, bathroom scales, pan balance, and string. For example, you would place the word **weight** on the bathroom scales. There are several cards with the same terms on them since there may be several tools in the center that measure the same thing. After you finish matching, ask your teacher to check your work.

2. Use your matching to complete your Rebus Guide sheet to use in the rest of the center. You may cut and glue pictures from the Picture Set for Rebus Work.

3. Select an object from those provided and measure it in some way. You may choose whether you want to use a scale to weigh it or use some other measurement tool. Use the pictures provided to write a rebus sentence that tells what you measured and what tool you used. There is a word bank on the sheet to help you. An example follows:

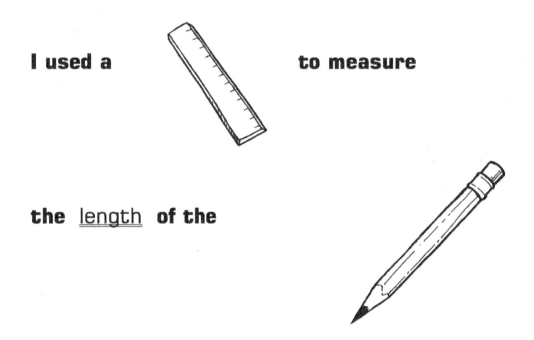

I used a .... **to measure**

the <u>length</u> **of the**

4. Select at least two more objects and write rebus sentences about them.

Card Set 1

weight	length
width	weight
height	length
width	height

Picture Set for Rebus Work

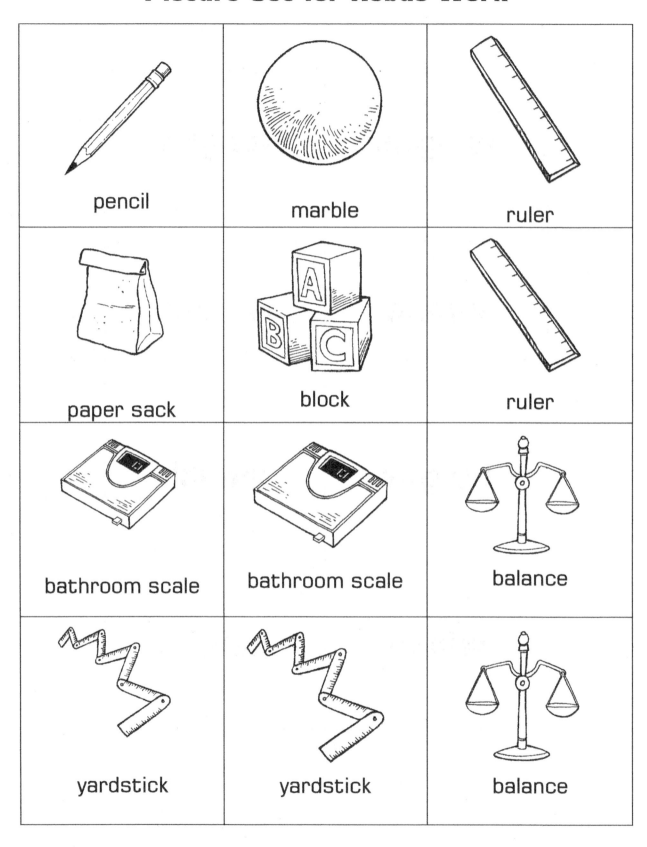

pencil	marble	ruler
paper sack	block	ruler
bathroom scale	bathroom scale	balance
yardstick	yardstick	balance

Rebus Guide

WORD BANK			
length	width	height	weight

I used a   to measure the _____

of the

I used a   to measure the _____

of the

I used a   to measure the _____

of the

➤ **Tiering the Center**

➤ **Older or More Able Students**
Three options are provided for this level.

Center Preparation
Students working in this center will benefit from information provided on a project board background, chart pad, or poster. The information will aid those who need help learning the appropriate mathematical terms of measurement as well as the names of the tools of measurement. The names and pictures of the tools depend on what is placed in the center. Following are examples of measurement terms that may be needed:

length	width	height	weight	cups
circumference	volume	inches	yards	feet
pounds	ounces	liters	millimeters	
meters	teaspoons	tablespoons		

Include pictures of objects described in several ways. Examples follow:

The book is 6 inches wide and 8 ½ inches long. It is 2 inches tall. The book weighs one pound.

The apple is 4 inches tall and weighs 6 ounces. The circumference is 8 inches.

The glass is 6 inches tall and will hold 5 ounces of liquid. The circumference of the glass is 11 inches.

Jimmy is 3 1/2 feet tall and weighs 55 pounds.

➤ **Option 1**

Objectives

1. The student will develop concepts of measurement.
2. The student will understand how to use various measurement tools.
3. The student will develop descriptions of objects using the language of mathematics.

Materials

1. Matching Card Set 2 – create on white card stock and cut out
2. Matching Card Set 3 – create on yellow cards stock and cut out
3. My Reference Guide page 61
4. Measurement tools:
   a. ruler
   b. yardstick
   c. bathroom scales
   d. science balance and weights
   e. measuring cups or measurement beakers
   f. string
   g. other tools as needed

5. Objects to measure (these will vary according to the child's age/ability)
   - empty coffee can
   - medium-sized wooden building block
   - box of tissues
   - roll of paper towels
   - film canister
   - other objects as needed

Student Directions

Do you ever wonder what a number stands for after you have measured something? Is it feet, pounds, or cups? Once you figure out what each measurement tools tells you, it will be easy. This center will help you figure things out.

1. Match the white cards in this center with the appropriate yellow cards showing measurement tools. For example, you would match yards with yardstick. There are some other white card words that could also go with yardstick. After you finish matching, ask your teacher to check your work.
2. Use your matching to complete My Reference Guide to use in the rest of the center.
3. Select an object from those provided and measure it in some way. You may choose whether you want to use a scale to weigh it or use some other measurement tool. Draw a picture of the object and write a measurement sentence that describes the object. Be sure to include what you used to measure it. Following is an example:

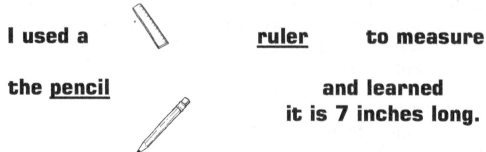

I used a **ruler** **to measure the pencil** **and learned it is 7 inches long.**

4. Select at least three more objects and write measurement sentences about them.

Matching Cards Set 2

inches	**feet**
yards	**pounds**
ounces	**millimeters**
cups	**tablespoons**
teaspoons	**meters**
centimeters	

Matching Cards Set 3

bathroom scale	**pan balance**
yard stick	**ruler**
measuring tape	**measuring cup**

Use My Reference Guide on the following page.
The questions students complete on this guide vary according to the grade level objective.

My Reference Guide

Name _____

Write your answers.

1. When I measure something with a ruler my answer

could be in _____, _____, or

_____.

2. When I measure using a bathroom scale, my answer

will be in _____.

3. If I use a measuring cup, my answer will be in

_____.

4. When I measure using a spoon, my answer will be in

_____ or _____.

5. Measuring with a pan balance, my answer will be in

_____ or _____.

➤ Option 2
Describing more than one measurement

Objectives

1. The student will develop concepts of measurement.
2. The student will determine multiple ways to describe an object through measurement.

Student Directions

How many different ways can you measure an object?

1. Select an object in this center and measure it in several different ways. Draw a picture of the object and write two measurement sentences that describe the object. Your challenge is to measure the object in as many different ways as possible. An example follows:

The chair is 3 feet tall and it weighs 9 pounds.

2. Complete this activity for several different objects.
3. You may also want to write some Object Riddles about things in the center to challenge your friends. For example, instead of naming the chair, the following riddle could be given.

**I am 3 feet tall.
I weigh 6 pounds.
My legs are 1 foot 1 inch long.
Who am I?**

If a friend guesses that your riddle is about a chair, ask the friend to "prove it" by doing the measurements.

➤ Option 3
Describing one measurement in several ways

Materials

1. Matching Card Sets 2 and 3 – create on white card stock
2. Reference Guide sheet page 61
3. Measurement tools:
    a. ruler
    b. yardstick
    c. bathroom scales
    d. pan balance and weights
    e. measuring cups or measurement beakers
    f. string
4. Writing Materials

Student Directions

How many different ways can you describe the same measurement of an object? For example, you say that a cup is about 3 ½ inches tall or that it is about 9 centimeters tall. Should you say that the package you want to mail weighs 24 ounces or that it weighs 1 ½ pounds?

1. Use any of the tools provided to measure one of the objects in this center. Draw a picture of the object and write two measurement sentences that describe the same characteristic of the object. For example:

The telephone receiver is about 17 centimeters long or about 7 1/8 inches long.

2. Complete this activity for several different objects.
3. Discuss how you would know what type of measurement unit to use.

➤ Younger or Less Able Students

Students who are unfamiliar with measurement should be allowed to simply explore how to use the measurement tools before being asked to complete a specific assignment in this center. The directions for this level might be "*Measure at least 5 different objects in this center.*" Change the objects to be measured in the center often.

Research in a Bag

Standards Addressed

Language Arts: The student gathers and uses information for purposes of research.

Science: The student develops an understanding of the characteristics of organisms.

Social Studies: The student develops an understanding of the characteristics and practices of culture.

Objectives

1. The student will use multiple sources to gather information addressing specific research questions.
2. The student will summarize information gathered from a variety of sources.

Materials

1. Nonfiction books pertaining to topic(s)
2. Visual information on topic (if available)
   - Picture books
   - Periodicals and magazines
   - Calendars with pictures pertaining to topic(s)
   - Photographs
   - Sketches
   - Videos
3. Computer and CDs
4. Sandwich size zipper plastic bags
5. White index cards (or cut paper to fit bags)

Center Preparation

1. Prepare a set of printed questions for each student. Although the questions will vary according to topic, and it is usually necessary for the teacher to write the questions, several are suggested below.
2. Students usually work in a research center over time. Therefore, plan for simple storage and easy retrieval of the research bags by individu-

als. Since students often misplace the bags in their desks or cubbies, you may want to keep hanging file folders for individual students at the center. Students file the bags each time they leave the center.

Student Directions

1. Cut out the research question cards and write your name at the top of each of these.
2. Carefully read each card so that you know what information you want to find.
3. Place each of the cards in a separate zipper bag.
4. Begin your research by reading and/or looking at the materials in the center that go with your topic, person, or book character. Do not just read to find the answers to the questions in your bags. Read to learn about the topic.
5. If you find information that helps answer a question, write that on one of the white index cards, and put it in the bag with the question. You will probably find several pieces of information that go with each question. Put each of these on a different white index card, and file each in the bag with the question.
6. Use the information you gathered at the center to write about your topic, person, or book character. Work with one bag at a time, and turn the information into a paragraph. Make the bag question into a topic sentence, and then make sentences to relay the information you found. For example, the question *"Who were the most important people in the hero's life?"* would become *"There were several important people in this hero's life."* Create a new paragraph with each bag.
7. Arrange the paragraphs in the best order so that your report makes sense. One of the paragraphs may serve as a conclusion; however, you may need to write a separate conclusion to end your report.

> ## Tiering the Center

> ## Older or More Able Students

Vary the level of sophistication of the research materials selecting more advanced reading levels and complex websites for those who are older or more able. While these materials are available in the center for anyone, work with more able students to assure the use of these. It

<u>would not</u> be equitable to ask more able students to answer more questions or to write a longer report.

➤ <u>Younger or Less Able Students</u>

Vary the level of sophistication of the research materials, reading levels, and provide more visual information for students who are younger or less able. In some cases, ask less able students to research fewer questions.

Research Materials and Web Sites for Younger Students

Research Materials and Web Sites for Older Students

Topic: Heroes

RESEARCH QUESTION CARDS

Who	Who were the most important people in the hero's life? Why were they important?
What	What are the things this person did that make him/her a hero?
When	Make a list of the heroic things the person did during his/her lifetime. At what time in his/her life do you think the person truly became a hero? Why do you think so?
Where	Name the important places where the person lived or visited. Why were they important? What did the person learn in these places?
Why	Why is it important for us to learn about this person? What should we remember about the person?

Topic: Endangered Species

RESEARCH QUESTION CARDS

Who	What other animals live in the same environment as this species? Are they also endangered?
What	What is currently being done to prevent extinction of this species?
When	When did this species begin to have difficulty surviving? What was happening in the environment at that time?
Where	Describe the best environment for this species. Where would you put some of the surviving members of this species in order to protect them?
Why	Why would it be important to prevent extinction of this species? How does the species affect other living things?

Topic: States

RESEARCH QUESTION CARDS

Who	Provide some information about the people who live in the area. What cultures are represented in the area?
What	What country or countries did many of the original settlers to this area come from? Why did they settle in the area?
When	What are some of the most important things that happened in the history of this area? When did these occur?
Where	Discuss whether the people in the area live mainly in cities or in rural areas.
Why	Why do people stay in this area to work? What are the main jobs in the area?

Topic: Current Events

RESEARCH QUESTION CARDS

Who	Describe the people who are being affected by this event. How are they affected?
What	What happened? Briefly describe the event in your own words.
When	Tell when this event took place and describe any other important happenings during that time period. What else was in the news? Did the other happenings affect this event?
Where	Where did the event take place? Would it have had the same effect if it had happened in some other place?
Why	Why is it important to learn about this event? How can people use the information from the event?

Topic: Book Characters*

RESEARCH QUESTION CARDS

Who	Describe the character and tell why he/she was important to the story.
What	What was the most important thing that happened to the character in this book? How did this affect the character?
When	Discuss the point in the book when the character made a decision that affected the rest of the story.
Where	Did the story take place in one location or did the character go other places? How did this affect the character?
Why	Why was this character interesting?

*It is difficult for students to meet the objective of utilizing multiple sources in research if the topic is a book character. Students could interview others who had read their book in order to generate another information source.

Background Music

Standard Addressed
Language Arts: The student uses reading skills and strategies to interpret texts.

Objectives
1. The student will demonstrate an understanding of content of the book.
2. The student will interpret content through music.

Materials
1. Feathers and Fools by Mem Fox (additional literature suggestions at the end of this section)
2. Two or more musical selections
3. Writing materials

Author's Note: It is not necessary to purchase specific musical selections for this center. You may use classical or contemporary music without words that you already have. It is difficult to find an entire piece that fits with a section of literature; therefore students may select a portion of a piece.

Student Directions
1. Read the book provided in the center.
2. Become a director who is producing this book as a video. It is your job to pick out music to play during each of the scenes.
3. Listen to a representative part of the first of each of the pieces of music and choose the one that would be best to play while reading the section of the book where *"silence hung over the gardens and the lake."*
4. Give the name of your selection, and describe why you chose it.

➤ **Tiering the Center**

➤ **Older or More Able Students**

➤ **Option 1**

Student Directions
1. Read the book provided in the center.
2. Select the words below that best describe your feelings as you read the section of the book where *"silence hung over the gardens and the lake."* Use at least two of the words to write a brief description of your feelings. You may add other words of your own.

shocked	disappointed
amazed	disgusted
concerned	saddened
crushed	angry

3. Become a director who is producing this book as a video. It is your job to pick out music to play during each of the scenes.
4. Listen to a representative part of the first of each of the pieces of music and choose the one that seems to fit best to play with your description of your feelings. You may want to try reading your written description while the music is playing.
5. Write the name of your selection under your written description.

➤ **Option 2:**

Students who need more challenge can complete all the steps for Student Directions Option 1 using the following more advanced vocabulary from which to select descriptive words.

traumatized	disillusioned
astonished	aghast
apprehensive	dismayed
crushed	irate

➤ Younger or Less Able Students

Center Preparation

Tape record the book.

Student Directions

1. Read along as you listen to the tape recording of the book.
2. The saddest part of the book seems to be the section in which *"silence hung over the lake and garden."* Look at the picture that goes with these words.
3. Circle two of the words below that describe your feelings when you read the saddest part of the book.

unhappy	worried
mad	sorry

4. Listen to the first part of both of the music selections in this center and decide which of these go best with this picture.

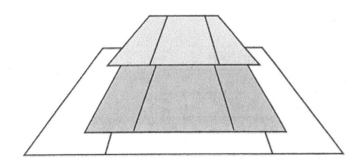

Additional Appropriate Literature Selections

Arranged in Order of Difficulty

Book	Author	Section
Where the Wild Things Are	Sendak	*"Let the wild rumpus start."*
The Tickleoctopus	Wood & Wood	*"For the first time in the history of people . . . someone played."*
Rabbit and Moon	Wood	*"Crane still walks on stretched-out legs, much longer than the legs of other birds. He is tall and proud, and he still wears a red headdress."*
Emma's Rug	Say	*"The rug had shriveled. It was ragged. All the fluff was gone. It was very, very clean. Emma cried out."*
Sister Anne's Hands	Lorbiecki	*"She had us singing and clapping and stomping our feet while learning our two plus twelve and six minus three."*
The Yellow Star	Deedy	*"The following morning the King of Denmark, with courage and defiance, rode alone through Copenhagen."*

Characterology*

Author's Definition: the science of studying the nature of a past or present human being or a literary character

Author's Note: There are numerous versions of the "I" poem in educational literature; however, an original source could not be located. The various poem formats for Characterology are adaptations of the "I" poem.

Standards Addressed

Language Arts: The student uses reading skills and strategies to interpret texts.

Social Studies: The student develops an understanding of the characteristics and practices of a democratic society.

Objective

The student will develop skills of character analysis.

Materials

Set 1 (for a center based on fiction or non-fiction literature)
1. Writing materials
2. Drawing materials (optional)
3. A book or tape recording of the book
4. A copy of the Character Poem Format (Adapted from an "I" poem, author unknown)

Set 2 (for a center based on a past or present human being)
1. Written or tape recorded information about the person
2. A picture of the person (if available)
3. Writing materials
4. Drawing materials (optional)

Student Directions

1. Read or listen to the book or information provided in the center.
2. If this is a nonfiction book, choose the character you want to analyze.
3. Use the Character Poem Format to write about the person or character.
4. Use the drawing materials to create a symbol representing the person or character.

Character Symbol

Character Poem Format

She (He) is

_____ and _____
(two words that describe the person).

Her (his) friend is _____
(This line may be left out.).

She (He) likes _____.

She (He) has trouble when _____.

But, _____
(tell what happens after the trouble).

Then, she (he) is _____
(describe the person's feelings at the end).

She (He) is _____
(person's name).

Character Poem - Examples
Based on Children's Literature

Lottie's New Beach Towel by Petra Mathers

She is
nice and helpful
She likes the beach and the lake.
She has trouble when Herbie's boat motor won't start.
But, she uses her new beach towel as a sail and the wind blows
them to shore.
Then, she is glad.
She is
Lottie

Rabbit and Moon

He is
brown and strong
He seems to like the moon and the earth.
He has trouble trying to get to the moon.
But, he finally gets help from Crane.
Then, he is happy.
He is
Rabbit

Character Poem Example
Based on a Famous Individual

He was
tall and had a beard.
He liked to read
He had trouble when he wanted to free the slaves.
But he was finally able to do it.
Then, he was satisfied.
He was
Abraham Lincoln.

Examples of Character Poem Riddles

Students may create riddles for other classmates by leaving the last line of the poem blank.

She is
beautiful and caring.
Her friends are dwarfs.
She likes to take care of them.
She has trouble when she bites into an apple.
But, she gets a kiss.
Then, she is very happy.
She is

_____.

Answer: Snow White

She is
little and blonde
She likes to explore.
She has trouble when she goes in someone's house.
But, she has to leave.
Then, she is upset.
She is

_____.

Answer: Goldilocks

They are
Short and round
Their friends are each other.
They like to eat.
They have trouble when they build houses.
Then, they learn the hard way.
They are scared.
They are

_____.

Answer: The Three Little Pigs

➢ **Tiering the Center**

➢ <u>**Older or More Advanced Students**</u>

The Advanced Character Poem Format on page 82 asks students to think more deeply about a person and creates an appropriate modification for this center.

<u>Notes for Tiered Activities</u>

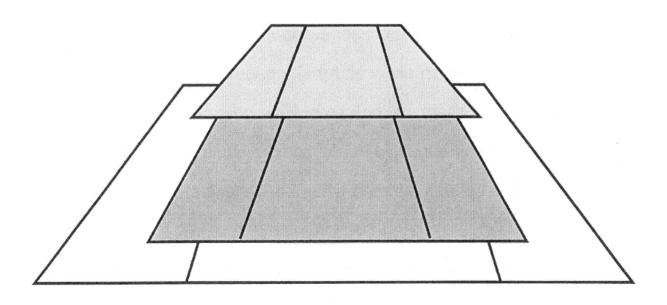

Advanced Character Poem Format

He (she) is

_____ _____ _____
3 nouns/adjectives which describe the character

_____
a complete sentence about 1 or 2 things the character seems to like

_____
a sentence that describes something that is important to the character

_____
a phrase that tells something the character worries about or has trouble with; begin with **He (she)** and end with a comma

_____
a phrase that tells how the character feels when he or she handles the worry or trouble – begin the phrase with **but he or she**

He (she) is _____ (the character's name)

_____ (the character's name) is _____
(a word describing the character)

Example Based on Advanced Character Poem Format

He was

artistic and creative and imaginative

He liked to draw and make people laugh.

It was important for him to create new characters.

He probably worried about whether people would like his cartoons,

but he was pleased when they were a hit.

He is Walt Disney

Mr. Disney was innovative.

➤ Younger or Less Advanced Students

Use the following Simple Character Poem Format.

_____

Name of Character

_____

(an adjective that describes how the person looks)

He (She) can _____

(something the person can do)

He (she) feels _____

(one or two adjectives that describe the characters feelings)

when _____

(place in story when character felt this way).

He (she) is

_____

Name of the Character

It's Inclined

Standard Addressed
Science: The student uses scientific inquiry to gather information.

Objectives

1. The student will develop an understanding of cause and effect.
2. The student will collect, record, and display data in bar graphs.

Materials

1. Round objects such as marbles or large beads
2. Cylinders such as those from paper towels, wrapping paper, poster containers, and/or laminating film to be used as an inclined plane
3. Several boxes of crayons or cassette boxes to use as standard measures of height
4. Yardsticks
5. Copies of the bar graph for students to complete

Student Directions
1. Choose a cylinder and a round object for your experiment.
2. Work on the floor in an open area.
3. Place one end of the cylinder on top of two of the stacked boxes provided to make an incline.
4. Let the round object roll down the incline through the cylinder and measure how far past the end of the cylinder it rolls.
5. Write down the number of boxes used and the distance the object rolled.
6. Repeat steps 3-5 once or twice more using the same number of boxes to be sure you have about the right distance an object would roll. You can average the three measurements if you want.
7. Then place the end of the cylinder on four boxes and repeat steps 3-6.
8. Next, place the cylinder on six boxes and repeat the steps.
9. When you have completed your measurements at different heights, fill in the bar graph provided with the information you recorded.

10. Compare your findings with those of other students who used the same cylinder and round object.

> ## ➤ Tiering the Center

> ## ➤ Older or More Able Students

Objectives

1. The student will develop an understanding of cause and effect.
2. The student will collect, record, and display data in bar graphs.
3. The student will demonstrate an understanding of variables.

Materials

1. Round objects such as marbles or large beads
2. Two or more cylinders with similar circumferences but different lengths such as a paper towel roll and a wrapping paper roll (larger, most stable cylinders can be obtained by altering the length of cylindrical mailing tubes)
3. Several boxes of crayons or cassette boxes to be used as standard measures of height
4. Yardsticks
5. Copies of the bar graph for students to complete

Student Directions

1. Choose the longer of the two cylinders provided and a round object for your experiment.
2. Work on the floor in an open area.
3. Place one end of the cylinder on top of two of the boxes provided.
4. Let the round object roll through the cylinder and measure how far past the end of the cylinder it rolls.
5. Write down the number of boxes used and the distance the object rolled.
6. Repeat steps 3-5 once more using the same number of boxes to be sure you have the approximate distance an object would roll. You can average the measurements if you want. Mark this measurement on your graph.

7. Then place the end of the cylinder on four boxes and repeat steps 3-6.
8. Next, place the cylinder on six boxes and repeat the steps.
9. Now complete exactly the same exercise with the shorter cylinder. You will use the same round object and complete a second graph.
10. Compare your findings for the two cylinders. How does the length of the cylinder affect the slope of the incline? How does this affect the distance the round object travels past the end of the tube?

➤ Younger or Less Able Students

Additional Materials
    masking tape
    tape recorder

Student Directions
1. Choose a cylinder and a round object for your experiment.
2. Work on the floor in an open areas.
3. Place one end of the cylinder on top of two of the stacked boxes provided to make an incline.
4. Let the round object roll down the incline through the cylinder and put a piece of masking tape on the floor where the object stops.
5. Next, place the end of the cylinder on top of six of the stacked boxes and let the object roll through the cylinder.
6. Place a piece of masking tape on the floor where the object stops.
7. Use the tape recorder to record your findings and explain what happened in the experiment.

Bar Graph

feet

	1 box	2 boxes	3 boxes	4 boxes	5 boxes	6 boxes
17						
16						
15						
14						
13						
12						
11						
10						
9						
8						
7						
6						
5						
4						
3						
2						
1						

Advertising Police

Standard Addressed
Language Arts: The student uses skills and strategies of writing.

Objectives

1. The student will practice working with a team to gather information.
2. The student will determine factors of influence.
3. The student will identify assumptions.
4. The student will practice decision making based upon facts.

Materials

1. Multiple advertisements from magazines and newspapers (Select and number the advertisements. Since students work in small groups of three or four, the center needs about six advertisements.)
2. Random number generator (die)
3. Product Sheet A
4. Advertising Team Sheet A
5. Pencils

Student Directions

1. You have just been named one of the key members of the elite Advertising Police. The work at this center needs to be completed by your superb team. We are counting on all of you to find the real truth in advertising. Can citizens believe what they read in advertisements? Are we being duped by some advertising or can we always trust what is written about a product? Each of you will need the facts from the other members of the team in order to crack the case.

2. First, as a team discuss whether or not you have seen any of these advertisements before. Perhaps you have used one or two of the products they advertise.

3. The advertisements are numbered. Each team member should roll the random number generator (die) to determine which ad-

vertisement he or she will work with. If you roll a number another person already has, simply roll again. Each team member needs to complete the Product Sheet A provided for his or her advertisement assignment.

4. Upon completion of the product sheets, work with your team to discuss and compare the advertisements by completing the Advertising Police Team Sheet.

- Make a list on the Advertising Police Team Sheet of the products in your cases and the ways advertisers tried to persuade people to make a purchase. These may include ways such as making people think they will look better if they use the product or suggesting that you will have more friends if you use the products. Sometimes the advertisements don't say this in words, but show it in pictures.

- As members of the Advertising Police, decide whether you think the things on your list are the truth. Check **yes** if you believe what the advertiser wants you to believe is true, check **no** for those that you do not think are true and check **maybe** for those that might be true.

- Finally, write down the numbers of the advertisement(s) you believe are the most truthful.

- Sign your name at the bottom of your Advertising Police Team Sheet showing that you agree with the team's decision.

Thank you for your dedicated work on the Advertising Police. We're depending upon you!

Product Sheet A

Name of Product	Type of Product (food, toy, etc.)

Discuss whether the advertisement offers anything for free or at a discount.

If someone uses this product, what do you think is supposed to happen?

What does the advertisement say or infer about why you need the product? What assumption(s) does the advertisement want you to make? In other words, how are they trying to persuade you to buy? What do they want you to think?

Do you think the advertisement is telling the whole truth and nothing but the truth? Please explain why you think this.

Advertising Police Team Sheet A

Product	What the Advertiser Wants Customers to Think	Yes? No? Maybe?
		__yes __no __ maybe
		__yes __no __ maybe
		__yes __no __ maybe
		__yes __no __ maybe
		__yes __no __ maybe
		__yes __no __ maybe
Number(s) of Advertisement That Seem to Be Most Truthful		

Signatures of Team Members

_____   _____

_____   _____

➤ **Tiering the Center**

➤ **Older or More Able Students**

Objectives

1. The student will practice working with a team to gather information.
2. The student will determine factors of influence.
3. The student will identify assumptions.
4. The student will practice decision making based upon facts.
5. The student will consider how types of appeal vary by audience.

Materials

1. The materials are basically the same. However, the advertisements need to focus on products that appeal to various types of customers. For example, one might be for toys that appeal to very young children while another for DVDs might appeal to teenagers. The task sheets vary for this level.
2. Product Sheet B
3. Advertising Police Team Sheet B
4. Drawing Materials

Student Directions

1. Same as 1 - 3 of the center, pages 88-89, using Product Sheet B.
2. Answer the questions and complete the task on the Advertising Police Team Sheet B.

Product Sheet B

Name of Product	Type of Product (food, toy, etc.)

What does the advertisement say or infer about why you need the product? What assumption(s) does the advertisement want you to make? In other words, how are they trying to persuade you to buy? What do they want you to think?

Do you think the advertisement is telling the whole truth and nothing but the truth? Please explain why you think this.

Describe the customer to whom the advertisement is directed. For example it could be for people who play sports or for parents of babies. Explain how the audience for the ad affects the inferences made.

Advertising Police Team Sheet B

1. Describe why advertisers need to use different types of appeal for different audiences.

   _____

   _____

   _____

   _____

2. If an advertiser wanted to sell something to students your age, what ways might they appeal to you? In other words, what would make you want to buy something? For example, it might be important for them to offer you something for free with the item or to suggest that you would have more friends if you bought the item. Make a list of ways an advertiser might appeal to you.

   _____

   _____

   _____

   _____

3. TASK: Use one or two of those ways to appeal to students your age to create a new advertisement for a pair of shoes. For example, if the shoe manufacturer thought you liked ice cream, the advertisement for shoes might include a coupon for 5 free ice cream cones. Work with your team to create the advertisement.

➤ Younger or Less Able Students

Author's Note: Have young students look at advertisements and tell what is being advertised and what they like about the advertisement (color scheme, pictures, etc.) Have them tape record their comments.

The following tier is for students who can write some of their ideas.

Objectives

1. The student will practice working with a team to gather information.
2. The student will determine factors of influence.
3. The student will identify assumptions.
4. The student will practice decision making based upon facts.
5. Same as a typical center yet realized at a less complex level.

Materials

1. Same as typical center using advertisements that are very straightforward and simple.
2. Product Sheet C
3. Advertising Police Team Sheet C
4. Pencils

Product Sheet C

Name of Product	What is it? (Is it food or toys?)

What, if anything, do you get free with the product?

Tell what is in the advertisement that you think would make people want to buy this product.

Do you think the advertisement tells the truth? ____Yes   _____ No

Why?

Advertising Police Team Sheet C

Look at all the advertisements. Make a list of what you like about them.

_____

_____

_____

_____

_____

_____

Write the names of the products from the advertisements that your team believes they would want to buy.

_____

_____

_____

Elaboration Station

Standard Addressed
Language Arts: The student uses skills and strategies of writing.

Objective
The student will practice writing elaborative sentences.

Materials
1. Written steps for technique (see below)
2. Book or written materials about which basic sentences have been written
3. Set(s) of basic sentences-several are provided below; however teachers can also create other sets for pieces of literature, social studies information, etc.
4. Writing materials
5. Random Question Generator*

*Create the random question generator from a blank cube. Use a permanent marker to write the following words, one per side, on the cube: *Who, What, Where, When, Why, How.* Teachers can use the visual, page 103, for younger students or those who do not read. Prepare a cube and then paste the pictures on the cube and cover it with wide clear tape or contact paper.

Student Directions
1. Read or listen to a tape of the text provided.
2. Read the simple paragraph provided.
3. Work with one sentence at a time until you have completed the paragraph.
4. Roll the Random Question Generator and use the word you rolled to make up a question about the first sentence.
5. Rewrite the sentence to include the answer to your question.
6. Edit all the sentences the same way.
7. When you have finished all the sentences and put them into a paragraph, make any changes needed so that the writing flows nicely and makes sense.

Folktale Example:

The student reads the paragraph about the folktale.

Little Red Riding Hood did what her Mother wanted. She met someone. She got to the house. She was surprised.

Then the student rolls the random question generator and uses the word rolled to pose a question about the sentence.

Original Sentence	Word Rolled	Question Generated
Little Red Riding Hood did what her Mother wanted.	WHY?	Why did her mother want her to go?

New Sentence:

Little Red Riding Hood did what her Mother wanted because her Grandmother was sick.

Original Sentence	Word Rolled	Question Generated
She met someone.	WHEN?	When did she meet someone?

New Sentence:

On her way to Grandmother's house, she met someone.

Original Sentence	Word Rolled	Question Generated
She got to the house.	WHO?	Who lived in the house?

New Sentence:
She got to Grandmother's house.

Original Sentence	Word Rolled	Question Generated
She was surprised.	WHERE?	Where did she get surprised?

New Sentence:
But when she went inside she got a big surprise.

New Paragraph:
 Little Red Riding Hood did what her Mother wanted because her Grandmother was sick. On her way to Grandmother's house, she met someone. She got to Grandmother's house. But when she went inside she got a big surprise.

Does the paragraph flow nicely and make sense?

Edited Paragraph:
 Little Red Riding Hood did what her Mother wanted because her Grandmother was sick and needed Red's help. On her way to Grandmother's house she met a wolf. When she got to Grandmother's house and went inside, she got a big surprise.

➤ Tiering the Center

➤ <u>Older or More Able Students</u>

Use paragraphs that students must create information from rather than those written about familiar stories. For example:

The man in the street waited. He knew it would not be long. Then it happened. He would not forget this moment.

Janice wished she knew more. Her Mother did not tell her. She knew it would be a surprise. It made her worry.

Finally it arrived. James was excited. The day became interesting. His friends agreed.

➤ <u>Younger or Less Able Students</u>

Use simple paragraphs pertaining to familiar events in the lives of the students. For example:

I go to school. My class works hard.

My family lives here. We like to be together.

I like pets. They play with me.

I like to play outside. It is fun.

Additional Paragraphs for Editing
Based on Folktales and Literature

The Three Little Pigs

The pigs built houses. The wolf came to the houses. The pigs had trouble.

The Gingerbread Boy

The woman made gingerbread. She cut out the boy. He did not stay on the pan.

Goldilocks and the Three Bears

The girl went in the house. No one was home. She did not like the porridge. She found a good bed.

Eggbert the Slightly Cracked Egg

Eggbert had to leave. He had trouble finding a new home. He looked many places. Finally he found other cracks.

NONVERBAL RANDOM QUESTION GENERATOR

WHO?

WHY?

WHERE?

WHEN?

WHAT?

HOW?

References

Anaya, Rudolpho (1995). The Farolitos of Christmas. NY: Hyperion Books for Children.

Curtis, Gavin (1998). The Bat Boy and his Violin. NY: Simon & Schuster Books for Young Readers

Deedy, Carmen (2000). The Yellow Star. Atlanta: Peachtree.

Kilbourne, Sarah (1994). Peach & Blue. NY: Alfred A. Knopf.

Lorbiecki, Marybeth (1998). Sister Anne's Hands. NY: Dial Books for Young Readers.

Meador, Karen (1999). It's in the Center. IL: Pieces of Learning.

Pollacco, Patricia (1996). Aunt Chip and the Great Triple Creek Dam Affair. NY: Philomel Books.

Ross, Tom (1994). Eggbert the Slightly Cracked Egg. NY: G. P. Putnam's Sons.

Say, Allen (1996). Emma's Rug. Boston: Houghton Mifflin

Wood, Audry, and Wood, Don (1994). Tickleoctopus. San Diego: Harcourt Brace & Company.

Wood, Douglas (1998). Rabbit and Moon. NY: Simon & Schuster Books for Young Readers.

Goldilocks and the Three Bears (any version)

The Gingerbread Boy (any version)

The Three Little Pigs (any version)